DazeD

Vanessa Morgan

Featuring Poems by Malik

authorHOUSE®

AuthorHouse™
1663 Liberty Drive
Bloomington, IN 47403
www.authorhouse.com
Phone: 1-800-839-8640

First published by AuthorHouse 12/28/2011

ISBN: 978-1-4685-0681-5 (e)
ISBN: 978-1-4685-0682-2 (sc)

Library of Congress Control Number: 2011961872

Printed in the United States of America

Preface

I had to start at the end in order to understand the beginning and somewhere in between I found clarity. The truth as it is and not what my deceiving eyes had been telling me. With clarity comes peace, love, happiness and most of all new beginnings.

Contents

They are Just Words

"I know for sure that what we dwell
on is who we become."
– Oprah Winfrey

Words

These words I love so well
Won't let me recite the stories I tell
I have a disability -it's the inability
To pronounce words correctly
In my mind I enunciate perfectly
But when I speak these words they betray me
I stutter and stumble
Become frustrated and mumble
So people think I am not smart
When I was young, that broke my heart
I love words and that's a fact
It's doesn't matter if they don't love me back
I will never stop reading them
I will never stop writing them
Because with words I can live my fantasies
Always have sunny days and sail the blue seas
With these words I can go back in time
Or describe all the images in my mind
With these words I can be who or what I want to be
And they can't deny the love they have for me.

My Story

I had to tell my story but I didn't know how because the
words were too difficult to speak.
I wrote them down and decided I would make them a
song.
Although the music was beautiful the words carried too
much pain;
And the music would not attach itself to the words so the
song did not take life.

I tried to tell my story through a dance and the dancers
would move to the spoken words.
But when they heard the words their faces were grimaced
and their bodies contorted.
They couldn't listen to the words and move gracefully
because the words carried too much pain;
And their movements would not attach to the words so
the dance did not take life.

So, I wrote the words in a book and I put it in my chest
and left them there…

Then the rain came and the levies broke;
All of my possessions got water soaked;
But someone found my words in the debris;
And started reading the words to me.

Don't Say That

Sit your stupid ass down somewhere!
You so dumb you aint gonna be shit just like your no good daddy!
Shut your moff don't nobody want to hear shit you got to say!
That's why don't nobody love you!
Don't you hear me talking fool?
I wish I didn't have no kids.

STOP your kids are listening!!

She read them clear and loud;
Until the words formed a crowd;
The words described so much pain and agony;
And no one knew the story was about me.

It was because our stories were basically the same;
The only difference was the name;
They were attentive and happy to learn;
That someone had written the words with concern.

Now, the words were there for the whole world to hear;
Which lessen the pain and chased away my fear;
The shame was disappearing before my eyes;
No more hiding; no more fear of being ostracized.

The hurt and pain I lived with so long;
I realized that day I hadn't done anything wrong;
I left it all in my book and walked away;
I would still be bound if the rain didn't come that day!

Teachers

I love teachers because they motivate
Take our minds and stimulate
Challenge us and watch us create
Teach us how to concentrate
Sometimes they have to regulate
When we learn, they radiate
Encourage us to participate
Cheer us on when we do something great
See our talents and cultivate
Develop our skills to communicate
I want the world to always appreciate
Our teachers whose jobs are to educate

Ill Equipped

When I was born my mom was barely sixteen;
She was quite surprised when I popped up on the scene.
My father wasn't much older;
After my arrival, he mostly avoided her.

He was a gang banger and a drug dealer;
Small time, but he thought he was real killer.
His mom was uneducated with no skills;
She encouraged him to stay in the game to help pay the bills.

He didn't live very long;
By the time I was two he was already gone.
I never had a relationship with his mother;
Too many kids of her own and she didn't want to be bothered.

Life for me at home was always a party;
People at my house eating and drinking, partying heartily.
By age four I could gyrate better than any Video Ho;
My mother and her friends encouraged me to do more.

I can't remember my mother ever reading to me;
I remember the talk shows and soap operas we watched on TV.
Education wasn't important in our world;
So I was an ill equipped little black girl.

Five and my first day of school was bad;
I was crying, angry and mad.
At home they called me Tee-Tee;
I was confused when the teacher said "Twana" and
pointed at me.

I looked around for the people smoking and dancing;
Loud music, talking, singing, and laughing.
I don't like this place they call School;
Wasn't for me; just wasn't cool.

The teachers grew frustrated with me;
My attention span was decreasing daily.
I didn't understand my new world;
Because I was an ill equipped little black girl.

They started labeling me;
The kids called me dummy.
They told my mom I had a learning disability;
And they tested me constantly.

I couldn't keep up with the other kids in class;
I failed at everything; I just couldn't pass.
My self esteem was so low;
But I could gyrate better than any Video Ho.

The second time in third grade in walked Mrs. Staley;
A middle age white woman who focused on me daily.
She said I was beautiful, special and smart;
With her encouragement I began to work hard.

She asked my mother could she work with me after hours;
Sure, as long as it didn't interfere with her Happy Hour.
Mrs. Staley took me places I had never been before;
With books, numbers, shapes, colors, and I wanted more.

Lord knows, Mrs. Staley was my savior;
I don't know where I would've ended up had it not been
for her.
She exposed me to a whole new world;
Where knowledge is liberating for a little black girl.

She Said, He Said

She called me and asked me to meet her at our favorite restaurant. She said she was depressed and really needed to talk. When I got there, she was already seated looking distraught. My sister is always upbeat and I couldn't figure out what this meeting was all about. When I walked over to the table, she looked up smiled as she fought off the tears. I was nervous, anxious, scared but I hid my fears. When I sat down, she said, "My job is getting too hard, the children are different, the parents are different, and the expectations are different. The state and federal requirements has limited my creativity in my classroom interrupting the natural flow of instructions. I can't teach from a script. I let learning take me and my students where it needs to go. I don't box Knowledge in because it is a freethinker. I can feel when my students connect with it I can see learning in their eyes. Hear it in the responses. I know when and how to turn the Knowledge spigot on and I let it flow over. In my classroom, it's never turned off. There's always something to learn. Their expectations are unrealistic. Every student is not on the same level but I know how to meet them where they are and take them where they need to be. How can I teach Advanced English when my students can't write a complete sentence? And, the paper work is ridiculous. They are kids not statistics. I need my time to teach but they won't let me teach. I can't handle walking in the classroom every day and not making a difference; not impacting children's lives; not shaping their minds. I think I am going to quit."

I was shocked. All she ever wanted to be was a teacher. She loves her job. I remember her telling me how she loved the school, the classroom, the board, the books, and the interaction with her students, parents and peers. She liked the energy the school created it inspired her to teach these young minds. Even as a child, she spent most her play time pretending she was a teacher. I searched my heart for the words to say but none came so I prayed a silent prayer and suddenly he walked up. He was a nice looking young man professionally dressed and he was smiling from ear to ear.

He stood at our table and he said, "Hey Mrs. D. How are you doing? Do you remember me? I was in your ninth grade English class about ten years ago. Looking back, you were the best thing that happened to me although I couldn't appreciate it at the time. I remember trying to cut class and you would come and find me. What teacher follows you out of the building? When I didn't do my homework, you would call my parents. When I didn't bring a book to class, you gave me detention. You were a trip Mrs. D." He sat down next to her and he continued, "That same year my parents divorced and when my mother didn't return your calls you would call my father. That was a bad year for me and you were one of the few adults that paid any attention to me, cared about what I was doing and forced me to be a better student. I hated detention so I learned to bring books to class. You told my father you wouldn't allow me to fail because I was too smart to lose and I heard you asked my other teachers to look out for me too. Mrs. D, long after I left your class I watched you. You would be the first teacher at school and the last to leave in the evenings. I would see your mini-van in the teacher's parking lot many days after football practice and in the early mornings when I was running track. I know you worked hard for us Mrs. D and I would like to think I was special but I heard you looked out for all of your students. With a tearful smile he said, "Mrs. D, you told me I could do anything, be anything if I worked hard and I believed you. I want you to know I graduated from college landed a good job and was having lunch with a potential client. When I saw you over here, I had to come over and say Thank you Mrs. D." He hugged her and left.

This time she couldn't hold back the tears. She smiled wiping her face with the back of her hand. All of a sudden my sister returned. Then she looked at me and said those words I wanted to hear, "I hope you're hungry because lunch is on me."

Too Hard

My father was a drug dealer and when I was eight I saw
him get shot down we were walking hand in hand when
a rival gang unloaded on him his hand slipped away
from mine and he lay dead on the ground my mother's
a CrackHead five dollars for a blow job looking for that
next hit my grandmother ashamed my father dead my
mother strung out three children with nowhere to go
grandmother decides to take us raise us stay away from
the drug dealers stay away from drugs stay away from
trouble I do but it's hard not accepting rides in their nice
cars always telling me I'm too fine to be walking but I
promised my grandmother that I wouldn't be like my
mother
Never graduated high school
Never married
Never worked
Never took care of her children
Never gonna be nothing
Never loved me
when I see her I walk the opposite way every once in
awhile my mother convinces my grandmother she will
quit using she stays a couple of weeks with us then she'll
be gone with whatever cash she can find one time she stole
all the food out of the fridge
I hate who she is
I hate what I might become
I hate the sadness, hopelessness, scarceness
my grandmother had my mother too young my mother
had me too young and the three of us have had to live

too hard my oldest brother gave up started selling drugs
he offers my grandmother money she refuses this teacher
at my school she seems to like me she told me I was
smart she knows my grandmother works hard she told
me if I ever wanted to talk she would listen and she did
I visit her after school a couple of days of the week I
found out she knew my father they grew up in the same
neighborhood went to the same high school now she is
a teacher I couldn't believe it I told her once my life is
so hard sometimes we have no lights no gas I know my
grandmother is doing her best but it's hard having nothing
knowing you'll never gonna be nothing.

She said, "Never give up! Work hard -giving up is easy.
Living with dignity maybe hard now but in the future it
will pay off. I stopped complaining. I read by flashlight,
eat cold beans out of the can, and wear the same five
outfits I'm lucky to own. She said, "Never let your
circumstances control your fate in life you always have a
choice." My choice - I'm leaving the hood, I'll make my
grandmother proud one day with the encouragement from
a teacher who knew how to reach me.

Colors

"Flowers attract bees and colors attract children so if we can send great messages through color then we have accomplished our goal." Charles Miller

Colors of Annie Ruth

My grandmother, Annie Ruth, was married three times. Her first husband Charles was white as snow and he loved and envied her dark skin and full lips because she could never be mistaken for anything other than what she was. She was comfortable in her skin. Unlike her husband Charles, he looked white but was called nigger almost every day of his life. High-yellow mother and a white father, he was too white to be black and too black to be white. Charles was handsome he looked like a young Errol Flynn but he was never sure where he fit in. The black men hated him and the black women loved him. The women practically threw themselves at him. Once he decided to court one of the women, they would parade him around like a first prize ribbon they won at the county fair and he hated it. When he would be alone with them, they were more fascinated with his good hair and good white skin and showed little interest in him. They played with his fine locks and stroke his white skin. His color always overshadowed him until he met Annie Ruth.

She carried herself like she was the queen of Egypt and he always admired her from afar. Annie Ruth was black and beautiful and she embraced her dark hue. She had an air about her; she was different. She wasn't like the other women all greased up. Hair packed down with petroleum jelly after being fried with the straighten comb trying to be like the white girls. She wore her hair in two nappy braids even to church on the first and third Sunday. When he first approached her, she wouldn't give him the time of day. So, he pursued her relentlessly and finally one day she agreed to let him court her. When he visited her, they talked for hours and never once did she tell him how good his hair was and how she loved his good skin. At the end of their first date, he found himself playing in her hair and stroking her dark skin. She thought he was foolish but she agreed to see him again. Her darkness was her beauty and it complemented his lightness.

They married when she was seventeen and he was nineteen. Two years into the marriage, Mr. White hired him to deliver his crops to other cities. Sometimes these trips would take him all the way to Atlanta and he was treated like a white man and he liked it. No nigger, no coming in the back door, boy was replaced with mister and he felt good; he felt free. He loved Annie Ruth but experiencing life as a white man was the one thing he couldn't share with her. So, after four years of marriage he decided he would move up north to start a new life. He begged my grandmother to go with him but she knew he would never be able to "pass" with a charcoal black wife and caramel colored baby. She allowed him to walk out of her life. She knew when he left he could never look back. It would be as though her life with him had never existed. Everything black would have to be forgotten and replaced with everything white. It was complicated losing her man to color. It would have been easier losing him to another woman because then she would have had a fighting chance at keeping him. Losing him to a better life was something she had no power over. Losing him to a world she could never know never be a part of broke her heart. Annie Ruth suffered with *my man done gone blues*. Loving him enough to let him go eased her pain because she knew if he stayed their love would turn to hate. Every month she would receive an envelope with no return address with a couple of dollars in it. She was sad but she didn't stop living and she never stopped loving.

He started his new life; traded the black and brown for the blond and blue. He loved his new wife but he loved the old one too. At first, he struggled with his two worlds and there were shades of gray. In order to move forward, he forgot everything that was black. Annie Ruth was always in his heart and his son was there too but he had to keep them out of his head. He prayed she would move on with her life. Find a father for his child and make another man a good wife. That's exactly what she did.

Her second husband, Robert, was as black as she was. He was a good man and although he was black, very black, he loved himself. She realized if he could love himself he could love her too. They had three sons together and he loved his sons just as he love Charles' son. Robert died ten years after they married and Annie Ruth started to believe she was unlucky in love. She was a widow; this time to a sudden death; the first time to racial separation.

Annie Ruth decided to take care of her four boys and work the farm all by herself. With her mid-wife work, the white children she cared for, and overseeing the hired-hands; she decided she was too busy for love. She didn't see it coming when Richard walked into her life. Richard, my grandfather, was light skin nowhere near as fair as Charles, but he was high-yellow with hazel eyes and sandy brown hair. They had one child together my mother. They stayed together until she died in 1968.

Charles heard that she was deathly ill and he made the trip to Social Circle to see her one more time and to beg her for her forgiveness. So he left everything white and went back to everything black. He was surprised that Annie Ruth agreed to see him and his black love returned. Annie had no hate in her heart for Charles. When he saw her, he was able to see multiple colors, not just black and white but he could see red, blue, yellow, and green – a rainbow of colors. He realized he loved her in colors. Charles was saddened when he saw her suffering and his loved turned blue. When he realized all the years he lived without her his loved turned red. He thought about the years they spent together and his love turned yellow. She looked at him and smiled and told him that she always had a place for him in her heart. With that, he left and went back to the white but he never forgot the colors of Annie Ruth's love and realized she had a heart of gold.

Annie Ruth –
Singing My Colors

I don't remember the exact day but I can see her now
standing over that wood burning stove. I hear the
rhythmic sounds of the pots and pans as she prepares
dinner. Her movements are deliberate as she pokes at
the wood logs to keep the fire at the precise temperature.
Lost in her thoughts she begins to hum and I know she
is getting ready to sing. I love to hear her sing. I see her
chest rise and fall and the expression on her face becomes
solemn as if she was waiting on her queue. I anticipate
the sound of her voice before she releases the words into
the air. *Jesus keep me near the cross*, she sang with so much
emotion. An electric current flows through my body. I
close my eyes and I can see the colors of the words… red,
blue, green, and yellow beautiful and vibrant moving
slowly in tempo with the song. Now we are connected,
I'm fixed on her. When I open my eyes, it is as though
I'm seeing her for the first time. Her skin is smooth not a
wrinkle, not a crease and it's the color of dark chocolate.
Her hair is as white as snow with silver streaks that sparkle
like stardust. Her teeth are so white and her lips are
full and together they form the prefect smile. She is the
prettiest woman I have ever laid eyes on and she singing
like I've never heard her sing before.
Grandmother, the song and I became one. She is singing
and I am rocking back and forth soaking in every note, it
has becomes my lifeline and I feel every word, every moan,
every emotion that grandmother breathes into it. I have

goose bumps on my arms. Where is all this power coming from? It has become much more than grandmother singing to pass the time away, it's taken on life and it is in the room with grandmother and me. I began to cry it's a new cry where the tears are running but I'm smiling and I look at grandmother and she is singing, crying my cry, and cooking on that old wood burning stove.

In the cross, every time she sings the chorus it's more powerful than the first. By this time I am floating on the words of this old hymn. "Sing Grandmama," I yell. If she hears me she doesn't let on. She is singing for me and her invisible audience and cooking on that old wood burning stove. I've never heard words that were so sweet.

Rest beyond the river, Grandmother finishes the song and my trance is broken. She immediately begins to pray. I can't hear the words but I bow my head and close my eyes just the same. I do hear her say, "In Jesus' name we pray." And we both say in unison "Amen"

Then I look at my Grandmother who is looking and smiling at me. I'm in awe of her and she seems to know just how I feel. Then I ask her, "Grandmother how are you able to sing that way?" She replies, "I'm auditioning for God."

That was last time I heard my grandmother sing. She died later in the year from complication brought on by diabetes. Each time I hear Near the Cross, I think of her and all the crosses she had to bear during her lifetime. I know that she found *rest beyond the river*.

Annie Ruth's— Colored Women

Color don caused me so much pain
If I weren't a praying woman, I'd be insane
I could hate because of the trouble color brought to me
But that ain't how God wants me to be
And besides, I happen to love my black skin
God took a little more time fillin' me in
Black women -we come in all shades
Put us all together- we look like a colorful parade
Different shades of white, red, yellow and brown
We should celebrate but instead we put each other down
We been caught up in this color thang too long
There are so many other important thangs to focus on
Just remember, there's nothing more beautiful than a
black woman
We are unique and we have to love each other as best
we can
Hold close your skin color whatever it maybe
And see it as a blessing as God intended it to be.

When my Grandmother Died

I dreamed in color before she passed away.
Now, my dreams are in black and white and I'm sorrowful every day.
My grandmother loved me unconditionally.
And, when she died, it almost killed me.

I withdrew, went inside myself as I did when I was a little girl.
I put blinders on because I was afraid to face the world.
The weeks after her death I didn't leave my home;
I sat in a dark room depressed and all alone.

I was lying in my bed when I heard someone banging on my door.
Then I heard my Aunt's voice before my feet hit the floor.
When I opened the door, she looked at me and almost cried.
Somehow she knew I was lost and alone since my grandmamma died.

She helped me shower and made me something to eat; she told me it was o.k. to grieve.
How my grandmother wanted me to live on, a thought I couldn't conceive.
My Aunt assured me that she would be there for me.
And I knew she would because all my life she had been rescuing me.

For a month, she came by every day.
She would sit for awhile; we would talk and right before
she left she would pray.
On Sundays, she picked me up and took me to church.
I don't understand why she loves me so much.

She brought me back from a dark place in my life.
Not even a blood related, she is my uncle's wife.
I've always admired how she has so much love to share.
Where would I be if she didn't care?

You Don't Define Me

Finally, I love who I am
This lovely brown skin that I have
This kinky curly hair I wear in its natural state
These big lips and almond shaped eyes I use to hate

At this stage in my life, I want to be me
No longer controlled by what people think I should be
No longer accepting the labels they place upon me
I'm strong, independent, submissive, loving, I'm free

There was a time I had no self esteem and many fears
I drew strength from my ancestors and persevered
I am not your whore. Your bitch I won't be.
I don't have to shake my butt to get people to notice me

I am a proud black woman free of your limitations
I won't be enslaved by your verbal degradation
You present me to the world as a one dimensional entity
When I radiate so much love and positive energy.........

Belinda Blue

Belinda Blue it's strange hearing from you;
It's been years since I've even thought of you.
You say my son has left you all alone;
And you think he's come back home.

Well Belinda Blue, I haven't heard from Ron;
And I am anxious to hear from my only son.
You should have known you couldn't be a mother and a wife;
You ran Ron right out of your life.

Remember Belinda Blue it was you who broke my heart in two;
It's ironic after all these years he leaves you too.
You took him from me and she took him from you;
He was only sixteen when he started messing with you.

Belinda Blue -He gave up his dreams for you.
He wanted to continue with school and not support you.
But you made him feel worthless and guilty;
After your criticism, he did what you wanted him to do.

Belinda Blue -He wasn't ready for a relationship with you.
You were the first woman he ever knew.
He was a young boy who was very confused;
And you took advantage of him, he was used and abused.

Belinda Blue, if you are calling for sympathy,
You are wasting your time on me.
For years, I begged you to leave my son alone;
Just leave him be and let him come back home.

Belinda Blue, my pleas fell on deaf ears;
You kept my son away from me for twenty years.
He wouldn't even call me on Mother's Day;
All because you brainwashed him and took him away.

Now, you can relate to the pain I felt for years;
Many nights my pillow wet from tears.
It was nice knowing you;
Good luck and good-bye, Belinda Blue.

My Aunt

She was my grandfather's favorite child;
With her blue eyes and great big smile.
She was the fairest of the six girls;
And Papa knew she could have the better of the two
worlds.

Papa knew she could easily pass for white;
And escape to a new life, like a thief in the night.
But once she crossed, she could never return;
She could forget the "colored only" signs and crosses the
Klan burns.

If you were Papa, what would you do?
Living in the south, in America, in 1942.
Being black ain't beautiful, it hard as hell!
And Papa knew the life of a poor nigger too well.

So Papa watches his little girl play;
She will be twelve on her next birthday.
She knows she is different from the others;
So much lighter than her sisters and brothers.

Many times Papa was asked, "Why you holding that little
white girl's hand?"
With his eyes affixed to the ground, feeling less than
a man;
He was always so proud to say,
"She is my daughter Sir," as he walked away.

My aunt's name is Bessie Mae.
She is a faceless white woman today.
Papa let Bessie go to the other world.
Where they are always nice to a little white girl.

Born Black

His body hung from a tree
For the whole plantation to see
She saw his body flinching
Rope on his neck pinching
It was her very first lynching
He wanted to be free
Leave this life of slavery
He was caught a few days ago
Beaten for five hours or more
Now everybody knows a runaway's fate
'Cause ole Massa won't tolerate
Anybody leaving and trying to be free
'Cause if you try you be up in a tree
The picture of him wouldn't leave her mind
Got so depressed she willed herself blind
She no longer wanted to see
The injustice and brutality of slavery
That was her son hanging from that tree
And ole Massa was his daddy
But her blind eyes could never disguise
The hate she internalized
Her people being dehumanized
Because they were born black
Always held back
Beaten, worked, lived in a shack
Picking cotton until their hands bled
Then have to beg Massa for a piece of bread
She didn't want to see the overseers
Grew tired of her own blood, sweat, and tears

Remembering the hurt from yesteryears
The children taken away and sold
On the auction block like black gold
She couldn't find peace
Wanted the madness to cease
So she prayed for her children's children
Time and time again
That they may be born free
And never have to hang from a tree

Through the Years

This chapter tells stories of people I've loved and admired and situations I have encountered through the years.

"What lies behind us and what lies before us are tiny matters compared to what lies within us." Ralph Waldo Emerson

DazeD

Sometimes life is like a maze
So many dead ends, walls, and delays
Can't seem to push your way through
Something or someone is always blocking you
Life hits you hard and you are amazed
That you don't fall just a little dazed
People coming in and out of your life
Bringing confusion, negativity, and strife
Finally you realize there's time for a change
Friends, goals, dreams are rearranged
The harder you try the tougher life gets
You keep on trying 'cause you can't quit
Your strength comes from somewhere
Maybe, it's because you know the power of prayer
You know that He's a keeper
You become a kingdom of God seeker
Many times life could have taken you out
But He was always there to bring about
A change in your journey an exit from the maze
Tearing down walls and by-passing delays
Now you are rejoicing heart full of praise
Next time in your maze remember
To always listen and surrender
He is there to provide direction
Comfort, love, and protection

He's right there by your side
Just let Him be your guide
He's a heavy lifter; He will carry you
No matter what you are up against He'll bring you
through!!!

Lord we need You.

Destructive People

They kill your dreams
They destroy your self-esteem
Only concerned about themselves
Your opinion has to be theirs
Won't allow you to grow
Everything you do they want to know
They take your power
Your soul they devour
They encourage you to do wrong
Want you to feel you belong
They won't allow your light to shine
Don't won't you to have your own mind
If you see them coming, run
Because destructive people will leave you numb

Jim & Mary – 2003

I was seventeen when we met;
A day I will never forget.
We fell in love instantly;
Married in 1963.

Everyone said it would not last;
We were too young and moved too fast.
That was forty years ago;
Just shows you what they know?

Jim was everything to me;
He died so suddenly.
Left me without a clue;
What am I suppose to do?

Loving him was my life;
I was proud to be his wife.
Then one day he's gone;
How am I supposed to live on?

When I graduated from college, he was there
With a great big smile and chest full of air.
In all my greatness, I was his clay;
He created this woman you see today.

He was more than a husband;
He was my best friend.
He believed in me and never let me quit;
I am the educated one, he had the wit.

Everything in the house reminds me
Of a life we lived so happily
And I've been so blessed because he chose me
Forever and Always: Jim & Mary born in 1963.

LC's Juke Joint/Rib Shack - 1970

I can't wait to get off and go to LC's Juke Joint/Rib Shack
Time I get there I'm gonna get a Jack Daniel with a water
back
I can't wait to take off this ugly uniform and pick out my
fro
Slide off these shoes and slip on my red dress and hit that
dance floor
I can't wait to hear Rufus Lee sang dem blues- he know he
can sang!
I'm gonna sit in the back eat me some chicken and a piece
of lemon meringue
Girl, I'm planning on dancing all night long and forget
about my work week
I'm so happy to be off I may give that low down Paul
James a peck on the cheek
Ain't nothing like dancing all night long with your friends
and having some fun
Because Sunday night will be here soon to bring in the
new week and it will be over and done!!

Addicted -- 1986

I am twenty-three and addicted to crack.
Every time I turn around some muthafucka's on my back.
This is my life I have to say
But that Bitch still preach to me every day.

Fuck-you momma you don't understand
When I needed you, you were with your man.
Get out of my face talkin' that shit
Go home and have your little fit.

Oh you care, now that's a muthafuckin' joke
When it was you that turned me on to my first smoke
I remember it well mother dear,
Little did you know crack would be here.

I just want to get higher and higher to forget this shit,
It feels so good momma, I can't quit.
So take your dumb ass on,
Don't come back, don't call me on the phone.

Thank God she finally left,
Now I can get high and be myself.
Last night I put that gun to my head,
One lil flick and I'll be dead.

Maybe I should leave that Bitch a letter,
It'll say Momma I'm dead and it's a whole lot better,
Than smokin' that pipe day after day.
I tried to quit but I can't find a way.

Momma! My life is out of control.
This shit I'm on eats at my soul.
I love you Momma, I know you couldn't tell.
I just can't keep living in this hell.

Faking It - 2011

Sometimes things get hard and I don't think I can't make it
My heart gets heavy and burdened down and I can't seem to shake it
I've gone through life wanting more and I realize I'm faking it
The more I have the more I want and they keep taking it.

The bills are piling high; spending twice as much as I've earned,
I am stressed which is causing stomach aches and heartburn
My wife keeps pressuring me; nice cars big houses is her only concern
She doesn't understand our finances have taken a downturn.

Trying to keep up with the Joneses was my mistake
Too many bills not enough money has caused me heartache
Just one more big money deal and I'll be straight
If not, we will have to relocate.

The Lottery – 2007

Before the lottery, she had three teeth in her head
With her winnings, she brought a new house, Mercedes,
and a four poster bed
She brought lots of clothes, jewelry, and four more new
cars
Threw big parties and brought rounds for people at her
favorite bars
Three million dollars is what she won and she told the
world
She loved the attention received when she displayed her
diamonds and pearls
The metamorphoses happened quickly right in front of my
eyes
She became mean, cruel and quick to criticize
She thought the money made her smart
What it actually did was change her heart
People began to avoid her
Friends, family, even her own mother
Then the money began to dwindle right before her eyes
To keep up the facade she started telling lies
Five years since the big win and her money was gone
And she found herself desperate and alone
She called me and asked for a loan
Told me she sold three cars and was trying to sell her
home
She couldn't afford it anymore
Moved back in the house she rented before
Instantly, I thought of all the mean things she said to me
The put downs, insults, and I became angry

But she is family and family is everything to me
I sent her the money quickly
She said she couldn't pay me back
Until she received a check for her income tax
During this process she lost much more than money
She lost family, friends, dignity and integrity
She didn't realize people who love you don't change
Whether you have three million dollars or two pennies to
your name

"A fool and his money are soon parted." Thomas Tusser

Eight Years – 2007

We were together for eight years
We had our share of heartache and tears
But nothing prepared me for that day
When my husband told me he was gay.

My heart hit the floor;
I screamed and ran toward the door.
He ran after me; held me tight.
But I asked him to leave that night.

How could he make love to me and a man?
This is something I can't comprehend!
Eight years of my life just thrown away;
On a man who didn't want to admit he's gay.

I turned on him, then myself;
I felt so empty, I had nothing left.
Why didn't I see the signs?
Was I so in love I blocked them from my mind?

I cried all night long;
Wondering where did I go wrong.
The next morning I couldn't get out of bed;
My face swollen, eyes puffy and red.

I thought about killing myself;
Those thoughts came quickly and quickly left.
Over a man, no I don't think so;
I love me, that's one thing I do know.

Life is funny sometimes you see;
I played the hand dealt to me.
But it was God who mended my broken heart;
Thanks to him, I've got a brand new start.

Growing Up Gay – 1973

He always knew he was gay
The kids bullied him everyday
They never included him never let him play
And when he tried to fit in they chased him away

He was a nice boy but he always looked so sad
The way they treated him made me mad
I never understood why they had
To always make him feel so bad

The kids would treat him so wrong
Hit him, threw rocks at him, he never cried always strong
To avoid them, he took the long way home
It has to be hard when you know you don't belong

He never wanted sympathy from me
All was required was my company
I was one of the few that treated him kindly
He told me once he would always remember me

Although time has separated us, I've never forgotten my
friend
He was being himself never meant to offend
I admired the courage he had not to pretend
Because loving oneself is the only thing that matters in
the end.

My Best Friend Dying – 1992

He has AIDs and he is dying;
God knows I am trying
To accept my friend's fate
This visit, I don't want to make.

Here I am in this room;
It's filled with so much gloom.
My friend is wasting away.
I shouldn't have come here today.

He is skin and bones.
I remember when he was big and strong.
Now he is so weak;
I can hardly hear him speak.

He wanted to hold my hand;
I backed up and ran.
I was afraid to touch;
A man I love so much.

I've known him for many years;
But I succumbed to my own fears.
I hate myself,
Because I turned and left.

I've always known he was gay;
I never had a problem until today.
I remember when he told his family;
And everyone rejected him, but me.

I am standing in this corridor;
Thinking about the times we shared before,
He became so deathly ill.
So many emotions I feel.

Thirteen months in that bed,
Everyday wishing he was dead,
Only being touched by latex gloves,
Nothing even resembling love.

I walked back in
Because he is my friend
And I held his hand
Until the very end.

The People he Hurt

How did we end up here?
This was the thought in my head
Funeral services for a man I hardly knew
Yet I heard about all the
Mistakes he made and
The people he hurt
His death was a slow and painful process
Which they felt he deserved because of
The people he hurt
Asked for forgiveness
Was it too late?
In this room I can feel the hate
Why are they here?
Why I am I here?
He is family
My sister insisted we show our face
I want to leave this place
Because I am surrounded by
The people he hurt
He's dead and gone
He died alone
No one visited
No one sent flowers or well wishes
Now they are here
No one has shed a tear
Come to be a witness of his death
And hope to cash in on his wealth
His own mother wouldn't come
Turned her back on her own son

Because she was one of
The people he hurt
Finally, it ended
No one pretended
They left with all his possessions
Clothes, shoes, furniture, jewelry
Fights broke out among
The people he hurt
Pulling, pushing, searching, roaming
Around his home
I feel so sorry for him and
The people he hurt

Finding Tomorrow

I turned away because that was yesterday
That was the last day he hit me
I can't stay and continue to live this way
This is my last black eye
My last bruised arm
Yesterday was the last time I jumped when he spoke
I turned away
Just in time for him to say
I'm sorry don't go away
But it's too late
I'm picking up taking my black eye my bruised arm
And I am leaving
I turned away
From yesterday
Leaving it all behind
To find a better tomorrow

Fire Starter

She is a fire starter
Her tongue is toxic
Her heart burns in her chest
She takes pleasure in others' unhappiness, sorrow, and
distress
She spreads the news like wildfire
Getting energy from whoever will listen
You can see flames in her eyes
As she regurgitates the black smoke
She is intrusive ignoring all the "do not enter" signs
Spreading the toxic waste
Leaving destruction in her path
Hurt feelings for years to come
No one can put her out. No one is exempt. Nothing is
safe.
She wants the smoke to choke you
Suffocate you with her tales
Of others' misfortune
Many hate her
But somehow she draws you in by her flames
The fire is tantalizing
It hypnotizes you with its colorful dancing flames
Calms you as you listen to others' pains
Forbidden stories taboo tales
You listen knowing
You will get burn
She smiles
Because she knows
She has you

In the midst of her fire
Burning the good in you Burning your integrity, Burning
your values,
Burning marriages, Burning dreams, Burning
confidences,
She watches you burn
Watches the flames devour you
Then she leaves triumphantly
Knowing you'll keep the flame going
Spreading the fire
Until it's out of control
It's too late when you see the destruction
The hurt feelings
The innocent bystanders
All caught up in the fire started by her lethal tongue her
rotten heart
But somehow you get blame
For the fire started by her flame
When all you did was tell one person and the fire was
attached to your name
And she is left smiling while she manipulates the game

James 3:6
*And the tongue is a fire, a world of iniquity: so is the
tongue among our members, that it defileth the whole
body, and setteth on fire the course of nature; and it is
set on fire of hell.*

Reminiscing

Sometimes I sit and stare into space;
Reminiscing about him and our favorite place.
He was the love of my life;
I hear he's married two kids and a lovely wife.

I wonder why I let it end;
Not only a lover, but a true friend.
Sometimes we let pride get in the way;
That's why I'm alone and unhappy today.

He was everything I wanted in a man;
An apology was his only demand.
If I could re-live that day;
I know exactly what I would say.

Affair

I knew he was married but I wanted him to be mine
When he looked at me it was like morning sunshine
He stirred up feelings in me that I have never known
I had to have him even if it meant breaking up his happy home.

He told me that the only woman he ever loved was his wife
Although he fooled around she was the center of his life
I am the better woman and I knew I could change is mind
I am beautiful, educated and honey butter fine.

After six months together he ended the affair,
He told me it was over and didn't seem to care.
I begged him to stay with me, we could be happy?
But he pulled away, angry, and threatened to hit me.

I was so lonely I began to take long car rides
I would find myself in front of his house looking inside
I could see him with his wife, son, and daughter
And I decided if I couldn't have him, he couldn't have the kids and her.

But after hours of watching them interact
I could no longer fool myself and accepted the fact.
It was just a fling. It didn't mean anything. He left me
And I left him alone to be with his family.

SOS
Save Our Sons

"We Teach What We Most Need to Learn" - Richard Bach

Mad-Lyrick

He was young, black and gifted
When he rapped, people were uplifted
At some point his dreams shifted
He lost focus and in life he drifted

His life was reproachable
His behavior was unbelievable
Living a life that was unobtainable
Getting shot or killed was conceivable

He was a sagging pants, tattooed, gold- teeth thug
Carrying a gun, hustling and selling drugs
He was fearless; he was smug
Never realizing the hole he dug

His mother prayed for him everyday
She reached out but he turned away
He didn't want to hear shit she had to say
Then she got a call late one Friday

She couldn't believe this was real
He got shot making a drug deal
She just thank God he didn't get killed
But he would never walk again life on wheels

Much to his despair
He thought by now he would be a millionaire
Instead he was under doctors' care
And he couldn't find his niggas nowhere

Distraught and all alone
He heard his parents say hold on
Family was always his cornerstone
'Cause all roads lead back to home.

My Mother's Eyes

If I could see myself through my mother's eyes
I would be the man I am supposed to be
If I could harness that light when she looks at me
My future would be bright and worry free
I wish I could live up to the light in my mother's eyes
Unfortunately, my life is based on deceptions and lies
Awhile back I stopped listening to my parents' voices
Got in too deep because of so many bad choices
Now, I am busted, broken, and betrayed
All because of my true path I strayed
But through my mother's prayers I saw the light
Now I am starting over and my future looks bright.

Stevie's Story written in six parts.

Part I - Little Stevie

I want to tell you a story
About my little boy named Stevie
He was three and as cute as he could be
And he died so tragically
My mother called and it was an emergency
I had to leave for her house immediately
So I asked my boyfriend to watch my baby
I was gone two hours no more than three
On the drive home, something came over me
I had an urgent sensation to hold Little Stevie
When I arrived at my house, a policeman approached me
He embraced my hand very gently
In a very soft voice he told me
My boyfriend hit my baby and killed him instantly
They were going to put him in custody
He asked was there any abuse previously…..

Part II – After Thought

I knew Michael three months before I asked him to move in with me and Stevie.
We were dating and seeing each other so frequently.
I really thought we could be a family.

Stevie needed a man around because he was becoming unruly.

And I really thought Michael was the man for Stevie and me.

Part III - Stevie's Cry for Help

Mommy, please don't leave me alone with him.
He's bad.
He hits me when you're away.
Mommy that's why I scream and cry when you leave.
He hits me when my Mommy is not around.
He says shut up and I try but I can't so he hits me harder.
My Mommy is not around to help me, save me, to hold me.
I am scared all the time when we are alone.
But this time he hit me so hard.
He told me not to move.
I got up to get my football.
He knocked me down.
My Mommy is not around and I am scared so scared.
I try to cry but no sound comes out.
It's hard to breathe.
I look around for my mommy.
She is not here.
Where is my mommy?
It's starting to get dark.
I can't keep my eyes open.

I need my mommy.
Where is my mommy?
Maybe she will be here when I wake up ……..
Mommy

Part IV - Michael

It was an accident.
I was trying to watch TV.
He reached for the ball.
The ashtray slipped out of my hand.
Hit him in the head.
I never touched this child before.
We had a wonderful relationship.
I am under a lot of pressure.
Looking for work and going to school.
I need peace and quiet.
I am so sorry.
I didn't mean to hurt Little Stevie.
Pamela please forgive me.

Part V - Stevie's Grandmother

I knew that boy weren't no good
Puttin me down for livin in the hood
Said he had a law degree
Never once did he fool me.

Talkin' bout he ain't workin for the man
He uses his head not his hands
Well that fool didn't work nowhere
Just sat around all day without a care.

My silly daughter takes care of that fool
She said he'll make big money once out of school
What school does he go to?
I asked a hundred times and nobody knew.

Now he don went and kilt my grandbaby
My sweet precious Little Stevie
If I could I would kill him myself
Instead I'll pray for my daughter with the strength I have left.

Little Stevie was a sweet chile
With happy eyes and a half smile
Now he lay cold and dead
'Cause a sorry ass nigga hit him in the head.

Part VI - My Sisters

Sisters, No one is more important than our children
So get to know your men
Before you move them in
And our Children's lives won't have to end.

My Son

Almost every day, I see him on the subway train
Weather does not matter, sunny, snow, or rain
He walks through and begs from the patrons
I watch him but I can't reach out to my son

I spoiled him, never disciplined him that's what sealed his
fate
Once I realized my mistakes, it was much too late
I never believed anyone but him and upheld him in his
wrong
Now he's roaming around the city of Atlanta on drugs and
without a home

When he didn't want to go to school, I never forced him
If he wanted to stay up all night, I let him
When teachers complained about his attitude, I dismissed
them
When counselors told me he had behavior problems, I
ignored them

My husband left because he couldn't bear to watch me
destroy our son
I thought I was protecting him; I didn't realize I was
causing harm
He told me if I didn't change one day that boy would
kill me
He does every time I see him begging, unshaven, and
dirty

"Excuse me, I'm homeless can you help me out with something to eat."
With his hand extended, he walks to the next person and repeats
When he gets to me, I look in his eyes but he doesn't recognize me
I give him a five, he says thanks and my heart cries for my baby.

Drugs

Every time I hear a police siren
My heart skips a beat
When I pass a police cruiser
I try to see if he is in the back seat.

He doesn't think I know
How he makes his money
I've known for quite sometime
And it frightens me.

I love him
But I despise
The way he has decided
To live his life

Fast money, fast women
Might get him life in jail
Hot cars, lots of guns
May just send him to hell

Stealing dreams, killing neighborhoods
Selling drugs, selling despair
I pray he turns his life around
Until he does, parents beware!

Who's in Charge?

Momma, who you think you talking to?
You don't tell me what to do!
I said I wanted those gym shoes,
So you can stop looking at me like you a fool.

Momma, you hear me talking don't front on me;
Give me your bag and I'll give the man his money.
These shoes just came out today;
And I ain't leaving them, no way!

Momma, I don't care how you pay;
I just know I'm walking out with these today,
I can't wait to show my boys my new shoes;
Man, they gonna be shocked when they get out of school!

One Bad Choice

I sent my life on a different course
When I made one bad choice
I was one of those young black guys people celebrated
I had a good job, no record, and college educated
One night at a party I had a few drinks – buzzed not high
Got in my car to drive home never thought someone would die
Not sure what happened, drove over the white line
You couldn't image what was going through my mind
When I saw that car and another entwined
Then came the fire and I couldn't believe my eyes
Cops came, I was arrested for DUI and vehicular homicide
I was once idolized
But now I am ostracized
Everything I worked for jeopardized
Never should have drove that car after drinking
Should have paused a moment for some rethinking
I was only ten miles from home
I thought I could make it safely on my own
Word to the wise- want to continue to live a life that's thriving?
Well don't ever think you can drink while driving.

It's Just Me

When I looked around, it was just me
Left the family who loved me
I thought school wasn't for me
Starting selling drugs to support me
Got me a nine to protect me
Front Line Solider that's what they called me
Hurting people who looked like me
Got locked up and nobody came to see me
Thought those niggas were down with me
When I look around my cell, it's just me!

How can we help them?

Harris- serving a life sentence for murder
Essam- shot in the face lost an eye because he took money
from a dealer
Larry- driving under the influence killed two people -20
to life
Patrick- killed in a shoot out

Tony- committed suicide
Henry- can't read
Erick- crack addict
Michael- shot in the back in a bad drug deal

HELP THEM!!!!!

Mad-Lyrick (Malik)

Poems written by my son Malik

"Search has become that thing that we lost and now we've found again. It's a Prodigal Son." Jonathan Gaw

Niggas

When young black kids are close friends
They say they are Niggas till the end
I used to thank it meant something
When I heard it from a friend
I've come to find out its leaving your partner when you get
to the deep end
Or leaving your partner when you can't see a win
Or saying you down for whatever when your words are
pretend
And yet and still I find myself using the word time and
time again
That's when I found I don't need no Niggas; I need a
friend

Don't Look Back

Don't look back that's wut my cousin Nuk told me shawty
Get a car and break the rearview mirrors off it
Don't let your past events effect wut you can accomplish
I'm still here but I could have been in a coffin
Dude who hit me, it's a lot of dudes want to off'em
Even if they don't, God will handle that problem
Still tend to see my memories and see them often
Like how I had a tracheotomy and still talking
With spinal damage with a chance of walking
Bad organs from when the bullets had bounced off'em
Tragic that it happened, family sickened feeling exhausted
Praying I don't get added to their long list of losses

That's why I tell myself Don't Look Back!!!

The road ahead is clear
I am smiling from ear to ear
Thanking God He brought me here
Got to live another year
No more being in the trap, I'm sincere

That's why I Don't Look Back!

9 Times Out of 10

9 times out of 10 gotta get my ass in wit a click dats ready
to blast
I'm in the street with plenty of niggaz so I gotta think fast
I'm livin' faster than a corvette with the gas on full
Some say I won't make it rapping but I know it's some bull
Cuz me and Yella got it sewed up we don't care wut u thank
I got my Pimpinville niggaz dat robbin the game like a bank
We been doing this so long- so hell yeah it's gonna pay off
I done put too much work in the game
For a lemon lame
To look at me like he lost
But when I 'm the boss
I bet you recognize my face any day
And I learn from mistakes that's how I know I'm going to
get major pay
In The A
Where I stay
I wouldn't have it no other way
And it still aint no sunshine
'Cause we tote nines
And we rob everyday
And that's how it is in the L-Town u can't have no fears
I was raised a little nappy headed nigga
Pullin' triggers
And niggaz been doin' this for years

Gotta put it in gear
Won't be a better place to do it but here
And the rap game needs a nigga like me
'Cause realness is what they need to see

Malik wrote this rap when he was seventeen years old. I wished I would have read it back then. We need to listen to our children.

Yella a.k.a Kenneth is currently in Macon State Prison serving 8 to 15 for assault with a deadly weapon and armed robbery.

Warning Signs

Warning signs I didn't even pay attention to mine/
because I was to focused on my illegal grind/
but now that I look back on my whole situation I didn't
take none of it serious until I was almost dying/ So I
want to take time right now to mention only two of my
multiple warning signs/ the first one for instance is the
place where I trapped and did crimes on Shield Road
and the Shield Center was the name of the place where
I went for rehabilitate my spine/ and the second one was
when I heard bullets ejected from a gun I always felt a
few of them woud be mine/ that's why I should have paid
attention to my Warning signs/

Da Hard Youth

Being Hard ain't about being a gangster nigga
Being Hard is about overcoming life's obstacles
I felt it was over but back then I wasn't thinking
I was becoming a victim of governmental temptation
Money, Sex and Drugs is ruining a great nation
Our youth losing work ethnic from computers and play-
stations
But, get them a play-station; the new PS3s is cool
Freedom is good information that will keep them in
school
Make them remember knowledge is power and not to
follow fools
They are our creation -treat them like they sacred
The secret to planting seeds is how you grow it and raise it.

I am Me

Every day at school people say
"Giirrlll, look at you! You are so ugly!"
Please
In their eyes, I'm the ugly duckling
But in my eyes, I'm a swan
I'm a Princess in God's Kingdom
My mother and father's ultimate creation
I'm the best
I'm beautiful
I am Me!!!!

By Portia Durden
Granddaughter

Acknowledgements

I would like to thank all the people who supported I Go Hard and gave me so much positive feedback which gave me the courage to publish DAZED. So here I go:

Anthony & Paula Booker, Mark & Gena Major, and James & Sarahann Pease the first to read I Go Hard outside of my immediate family. Thanks for your support.

Sonji Lee organized my first book signing at her church. Thanks Sonji for pushing me out of my comfort zone. You are so special to me.

Marvette Critney hosted my first book reading/signing at her home. Marvette you are the best!

Kesha "Keke" Henderson recognized I Go Hard purpose before it was published. Thanks, I love you Girl!!

Much Love to my aunts and uncle: Edna Dallas-Morgan, Eloise Hinesman-Morgan, Minnie Morgan and Hiram Morgan Jr.

Debbie Waters-Lowery, Mary Bradley, James Reed, Leila Banks, Rita Semien and Gregory V. Jones my first co-workers to read the book. Thanks Ladies and Gentlemen.

Joyce Carter one of the few people who knew what was really going on in my family. Thanks Joyce for your friendship and loyalty. My family loves you!!!

Marlene Craig-Tucker – Thank you for supporting our (my son and I) upcoming project. Believing in us means so much!!!

My first cousins – Deborah Moye, H.James Dallas, and Billy Harris thanks for your words of encouragement it meant so much to me. Love y'all!

Sydni Booker my favorite little cousin. Thanks for helping me with Facebook. Love ya!

Finally – Thanks to my family:
Clarice and Ed Derricho – Clarice thanks for being my number one motivator. Ed thanks for helping step outside the box. E.J. my number one nephew.

My niece Amber Derricho - Thanks for reading my poems. I love you girl!

My mother, Ola Morgan, thanks for your encouragement.

My children Barnard Jr., Shante, Jimmy, Portia, Jimmeria and Mekhi.

My in-laws Amos and Elizabeth McCants.

My husband Barnard who is my bright light in life. Thanks for always letting me be me!!!

Edited by: Judah's Writings Unlimited